Published by Sellers Publishing, Inc.

Text and illustrations copyright © 2011 Jill Seale

Sellers Publishing, Inc.
161 John Roberts Road, South Portland, Maine 04106
Visit our Web site: www.sellerspublishing.com
E-mail: rsp@rsvp.com

ISBN: 13: 978-1-4162-0624-8

10 9 8 7 6 5 4 3 2 1

Printed and bound in China.

STARK RAVING MOTHERHOOD

A Mother's Pledge to Do It All!

Written and Illustrated
by
Jill Seale

SELLERS
PUBLISHING

This book is dedicated to my mom
who taught me the art of
mothering by the seat of your pants
and that sometimes
laughing is as important as breathing.

Jill Seale

To: _____

From: _____

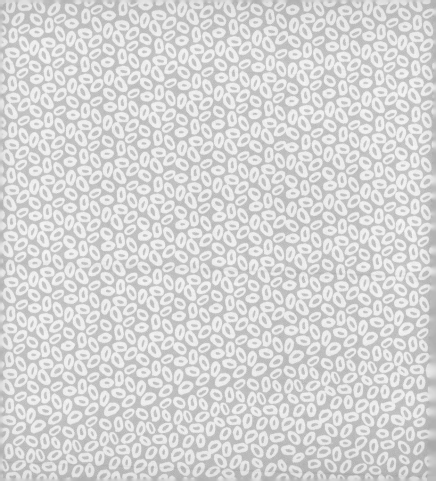

On my honor, I will try to do my duty for my home and my family...

to help find socks,

WHERE'S SOCKO?

make sure everyone
is outfitted
with clean underwear,

and pack lunches.

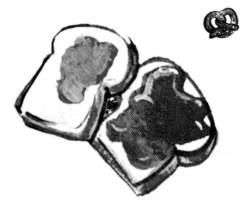

I will read school memos,

The Black Hole

attend after-school meetings,

shuttle to baseball practice,

carpool,

Miss Belinda's
Dance Academy

(tap
'til you
drop)

Little League
Division 1, 2nd Place

(and we would've won if
Lee hadn't split his pants
chasing a fly ball)

OUR TEAM KICKS GRASS
OUR TEAM KICKS GRASS

Green Dragons

PeeWee Football

Worthington Golf School
(lets kids drive golf carts
as soon as they can
reach the pedals)

make costumes for the school play,

then one foggy Christmas Eve...

help with the book drive,

Curious Boyd Plays with Matches

Hairless Potter and the

and make (and keep)
all doctor and dental
appointments.

I'll help build a life-size
papier mâché velociraptor
project,

From the kitchen of: Karol

Velociraptor (secret Family Recipe)
1 bag leftover whole-wheat flour
  that no one will eat
1 bucket water, Sunday newspaper
Glob of chicken wire in shed
pinch of salt
1 can grey garage floor paint
Dad's athletic socks to
  hide sharp ends of chicken
Patience!!

REALLY and TRULY read all school memos,

GHOSTS OF MEMOS PAST

Volunteer form
SCHOOL...
BE...

DEADLINE
2 WEEKS
ON $60

☐ YES!
☐ I'D BE DELIGHTED!
☐ ...IF I HAVE TO...

ORGANIZE LIBRARY
BEFORE REPORT
CARD WILL BE
ISSUED

be on-call 24/7 for any sniveling complaint,

spay and neuter all pets,

decorat
for a

initiate a "Glove Shack" mitten drive,

he house
olidays,

stitch up the heinie on all split stuffed animals,

change out seasonal clothes,

SQUEEZE OUT ONE MORE SEASON

SUMMER

WINTER

HAND-ME-DOWNS FROM COUSINS BILLY + ANDREW TO GROW INTO

SUMMER CLOTHES HELD ASIDE FOR CHRISTMAS AT GRANDMA'S IN FLORIDA

TOOO CUTE TO EVER GET RID OF

join the PTA,

and take
the scouts caroling at
the senior center.

Begrudgingly I will manage home repairs,

toothbrush out grout (have you ever seen such sparkling grout?)

no more wobbling toilet seats!

routine active lint-trap maintenance

whole-house light-bulbery

toothbrush out fabric softener residue

do my best with third-grade math and beyond,

try to maintain composure while failing at third-grade math and beyond,

and clean out the van at least once a quarter.

If I can locate them, I will try to return all library books on time,

Congratulations! We're naming the new wing of the library after your generous overdue contributions through the years!

notice floater pants on growing daughter and try not to pretend they are capris,

not scream at my children
n frustration, remembering I
vas once a kid and was just
the same if not more so,

and be the pack mule for vacation day-trip needs.

Things "rediscovered" in Purse:

Petrident Gum
wrappers are overrated!

"Bluey" Marble
from Childhood

Sock

Press-On Nail

Retainer
But whose?!

haul kids to piano lessons,
clean out my purse during
piano lessons,

Now do it 25 more times!

Chef Bla-R-Dee

the dog, "some"

Kids love to bite

Glazed Carrots
on the
OFF CHANCE...

and make separate meals for each family member to get everyone to eat.

Big Daddy Fat T-Bone Juicy + Succulent

Mom's Healthy Skinless, Boneless, Tasteless, Dry Chicken Breast

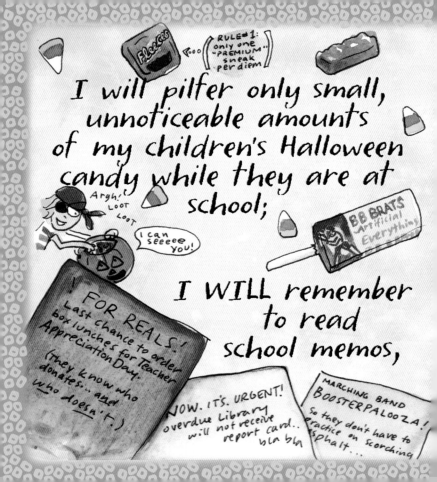

and try not to have an aneurysm over mind-numbing Dr. Seuss rhymes after the 400th time because I see the value in it for children;

I will not velvet-rope off my living room so that it may be lived in, and I will clean out my purse during dentist appointments.

← receipt graveyard

704-555-71 ...now WHY.te did I wrt this?

I will remember it's school picture day so as not to repeat the same hairicide my mother did to me;

(This was the start of my bad-hair life.)

be piano-practice enforcer, and not sit in scorching fear worrying that I left the stove on while trapped at school talent shows.

I will dutifully clean dog
slobber off of car windows,
use the toothpaste that
four out of five
dentists recommend,

I'll remember to use the clipped coupon BEFORE it expires (if I can find the coupon caddy), be manners teacher and enforcer, saying, "One day when you are invited to the White House for dinner, you'll thank me";

be homeroom mom,
birthday party planner,
caterer, cleaner-upper,
and
joyful hostess,

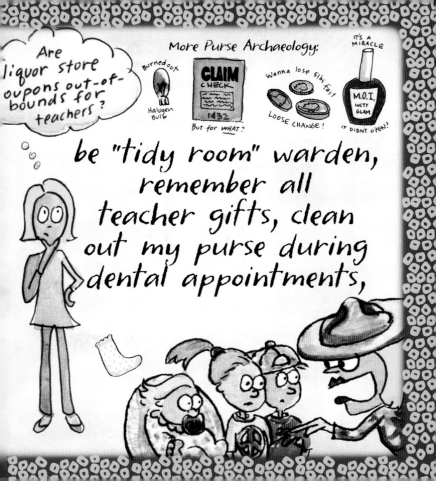

be everywhere at one time for everyone doing everything they need while talking the cat down from the tree,

Looook Mom! Look how I can balance on one foot on the deck rail!

actually look up from what I am doing and not just say "mmm-hmmm,"

mmm hmmm

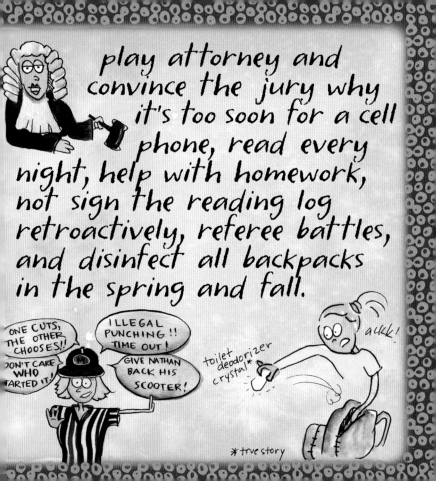

I will not criticize other mothers who manage to run a brush through their hair and a tube of lipstick over their yaps before carpool line.
oh Hiiiiiiiiiii... You look... greaaat!

and an occasional
show of affection from
my little darlings.